Armadillos
For Kids

Amazing Animal Books
For Young Readers

By
Rachel Smith

Mendon Cottage Books

Mendon Cottage Books
JD-Biz Corp Publishing

Read More Amazing Animal Books

Purchase at Amazon.com

Table of Contents

Introduction

The armadillo is commonly known in the Southern parts of the United States of America, as well as in Central America. But what many people from this area, especially the United States of America, don't realize is that there are more types and appearances to the armadillo than they think.

From tiny to huge, from looking prehistoric to looking cute, to looking like something that couldn't win against a pig in a beauty contest, the armadillo comes in many types.

The armadillo is truly a unique creature of the Americas.

What is an armadillo?

As mentioned, the armadillo lives in the Americas, North America and South America. However, there are most often found in South America. The armadillo belongs to the order Cingulata; a very long time ago, there were other families in this order. Most of these creatures were prehistoric animals. Now, only the armadillo family, Dasypodidae, exists in this order. Armadillos belong to the superorder Xenarthra, which includes anteaters and sloths as well.

A small armadillo (commons.wikimedia.org).

The armadillo is called an armored creature; this is because of their leather shells. The name 'armadillo' actually means 'little armored one' in Spanish. The Nahuatl, or Aztec, word for armadillo literally means 'turtle-rabbit.'

Armadillos range in size from the giant armadillo (up to 150 centimeters and 54 kilograms) to the pink fairy armadillo, which is about 13 to 15 centimeters long. The latter is also very cute.

An armadillo is a placental animal; this means that, instead of laying eggs, they grow their babies inside their bellies. The placenta, which is kind of like a cord between the mother and baby, feeds the baby from the mother's bloodstream and the like. Human beings need placentas in the womb, like most mammals (animals who nurse).

They have a low body temperature, like other animals in the superorder Xenarthra. This makes them well adapted to the hot weather of Central and South America, where they live. Also, they have a lower metabolic rate, which means they don't use up energy as fast. This is a very good thing because they eat termites, which are not high in nutrients.

Not all armadillos roll into balls. This is a common thing for several kinds, but not all have that ability. For instance, the giant armadillo is not the kind that rolls into a ball, while the southern three-banded armadillo is. It's a way some of them protect themselves.

The underside of armadillos is never armored. It usually has soft fur, and is completely vulnerable.

How do armadillos act?

Armadillos act in various ways. For one thing, some are nocturnal, and get their food at night.

A mama armadillo and her baby looking for bugs.

Some kinds of armadillos jump when scared, whereas others roll into balls. Many of them who have a lot of plates (or parts of their armor) can't roll up, but the armor still helps protect them.

Armadillos have a really great sense of smell, though in turn they also don't have good eyesight. They rely on their sense of smell to seek out food, and tend to use their claws to dig it out of the ground.

They also dig burrows. Their claws are great for digging, far better than a human could dig with their hands. Armadillos like burrows because they can hide from predators there.

Armadillos have a number of cheek teeth, which are kind of like molars. However, unlike humans, they don't have both molars and premolars, though these teeth mash things up just fine without the distinction. They also have canines (sharp teeth) and incisors (front teeth in humans). This is because they eat bugs.

They carry their babies for 60 to 120 days. However, some kinds of armadillo can keep their eggs from implanting for a while, so it may be even longer from mating that they have their babies.

Dasypus, which is a family within the order Cingulata, tends to have identical quadruplets. This is interesting because such a birth would be very rare in humans, but instead it is ordinary among these armadillos.

Other armadillos have one to eight babies who aren't identical.

Burrows are shared with the babies, but armadillos are solitary, so that means they don't share their burrows with other adults. This means that parents don't stay together after mating, and it is entirely up to the female to make sure the babies survive.

Baby armadillos are born with soft

The babies become mature at anywhere from three months to twelve months, depending on the species. This means they are able to have their own babies, and take care of them themselves.

Armadillos can be underwater for up to six minutes. However, the catch for them with going in the water is that they have to swallow air first, or else they will sink. This is because of their heavy armor.

When they are preyed upon (attacked or threatened by a predator) armadillos tend to either flee or burrow away. While their armor is a great protector, they prefer not to put it to the test most of the time. Considering that many of them can't curl into balls, this makes sense.

The history of armadillos and humans

Armadillos and humans have known about the other for a very long time. South and Central American peoples have eaten them for longer than written history existed in these areas, and they were considered a curiosity to the invading Europeans.

Southern three banded armadillo curled up in a human's hand.

One way that the armadillo is used by the people who live around them is not just for food, but for an instrument. The charango is an Andean instrument constructed using an armadillo shell. The back of the stringed instrument is made using the shell, whereas the rest looks a lot like a normal guitar. This is because the charango came from instruments such as the lute and the guitar. It's a native instrument, but was created due to interaction with European culture.

Charango players are called charanguistas.

The armadillo has also, in more modern times, proved useful to science. Thanks to their low temperature and their lack of defenses, leprosy is a disease that is very common and easily contracted by armadillos.

Other animals are like this, including mangabey monkeys, who contract it in a similar way to armadillos, and rabbits and mice, who only get leprosy on their footpads.

Leprosy is an ancient disease that attacks nerves and skin of its victims. It often means that the person who has it is disfigured (made to look different) from it. Back in Biblical days, leprosy was a reason to make someone leave their home and wander forever as an outcast. In modern day third-world countries, it is still a reason to cast someone out.

Leprosy is not very contagious, or easy to catch. It actually can only be caught by a small portion of the population, and doesn't spread easily.

A person can get leprosy from handling an armadillo, or eating armadillo meat, but this is still pretty rare. Nowadays, leprosy is treatable within six months of discovery, so it is not the life changer that it used to be.

This is in part due to the armadillo and the tests done on it by human researchers. Thanks to having an animal that caught the disease so easily, it was much easier to test what would cure the disease.

Armadillos got the disease when they were introduced to humans from Europe who had it. Prior to the Europeans exploring Central and South America, leprosy had not been seen in these areas before.

The nine-banded armadillo is also used for science for a different reason. Because it has four identical babies, alike in every way, those babies make great test subjects. In science experiments, something that's very important is to control every part about the experiment they can. If all the armadillos being used are exactly the same, then they know the results they get come from what they did and not from the differences between the animals.

There have also been stories of armadillo shells being so tough that when hit by a bullet, they bounce back and hurt the shooter or someone else.

However, these shells do not save them from being roadkill. Especially the nine-banded armadillo is a victim of being hit by a car. The problem for this particular armadillo is that it jumps up three or four feet when threatened, and this works well against other animals, but it only means they jump up into the cars.

Armadillos that roll up are also in danger from cars, because their shells can't protect them from the sheer weight of the car.

Nine-banded armadillo

The nine-banded armadillo is the most well-known among the Western world (particularly the United States of America). This is because it is the most widespread armadillo of all, and lives all the way up North in parts of the Southern United States of America, especially Texas.

A nine-banded armadillo.

Many, many years ago, long before humans wrote down history, the nine-banded armadillo only lived in South America. This was back when South America and North America were separated. However, when the Isthmus of Panama was formed, connecting the two, something big happened.

The Great American Interchange was what happened when these two continents met. Animals from North America went down into South America, and animals from South America went up into North America.

One of the animals that went up was the nine-banded armadillo. It has a wide range in the United States of America, though it is most common in Texas. In fact, it is the Texas state small mammal. It only entered the USA in the 19th century, crossing the Rio Grande, a river in Mexico. However, they have been in Mexico and other areas much, much longer. Its range stretches all the way down to Argentina.

The nine-banded armadillo is so named because of the nine bands across its midsection on its shell. It's also called the nine-banded, long-nosed armadillo.

This kind of armadillo can't survive in very cold or dry environments, because it doesn't have much fat and doesn't hold water very well. It might become dehydrated (have too little water in it) if it lives in very dry areas, and that could spell death.

This armadillo is an insectivore, meaning it eats insects such as termites and worms. It's also nocturnal, meaning that it sleeps during the day and is active during the night. However, you may still see one during the day, as they have been known to move about then.

Sometimes, they will roll around on an ant hill, and this will force the ants to come to the surface where the armadillo can eat them. They've also been known to be attracted to carrion (dead animals) but this might be because they eat the maggots that form in the flesh.

Nine-banded armadillos are solitary creatures, and they tend to mark their territories with urine (pee), feces (poop), and special scent glands they have on their nose, feet, and eyelids. Females care more about specific borders and defend them, whereas males have larger territories but allow other armadillos more movement in them.

The predators of the nine-banded armadillo are animals like cougars, wolves, large raptors (predator birds) and other meat-eating animals.

The nine-banded armadillo can flee pretty quickly from a predator, but when it can't flee, it tends to dig a small trench and bury itself. The predator generally isn't able to get past its hard shell unless it is young enough that its shell is too soft.

Northern naked-tailed armadillo

The Northern naked-tailed armadillo is one of the two types of armadillos that live outside of South America. The other kind is the nine-banded armadillo.

It is a smaller armadillo, only 31-42 centimeters long, and it weighs a mere 2 to 3.5 kilograms. However, this doesn't make it easy prey; it still has the armor of an armadillo and is able to protect itself in similar ways.

This armadillo lives mostly in Central America and the top of Southern America. It doesn't have nearly as wide a range as the nine-banded armadillo.

Unlike other armadillos, its bands across its middle are not very distinct. It also has rather square-shaped scutes, or pieces of the armor. It has five claws per foot, and the middle one is enlarged and has a sort of sickle shape to it.

This kind of armadillo is rarely spotted. It may be that it is kind of patchy in its distribution, or that it hides well. No one is sure quite how many there are due to the rarity of sightings.

When it is caught, it is very loud, squealing and such to scare away the humans who have caught it. Also, it tends to pee and poop all over the captors, in an attempt to make them let it go.

They only have one baby at a time, and this baby is cared for by the mother. She has to pay close attention, because the baby is blind, deaf, and hairless at birth. Their armor is also very soft, or else it would be very hard to give birth to it. Much like hedgehog babies' spikes are soft when they are born, so too is this armadillo's baby.

Greater fairy armadillo

The greater fairy armadillo is the only one of its genus, and it is also known as either Burmeister's armadillo or the Chacoan fairy armadillo.

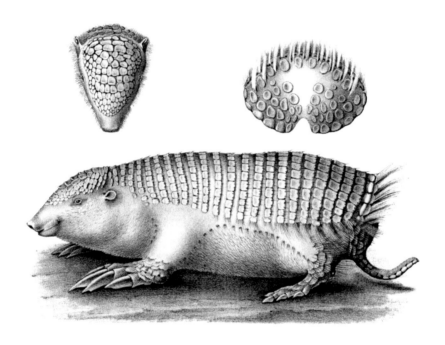

An old drawing of a greater fairy armadillo (commons.wikimedia.org).

The greater fairy armadillo lives in Argentina, Bolivia, and Paraguay. It likes subtropical or tropical dry shrub land to live in, and its home is threatened by habitat loss. This means humans are destroying its habitat, and this puts it in danger of not having a home.

When an animal doesn't have a home, it either adapts to urban life among humans, or it dies out. The greater fairy armadillo cannot adapt to urban life, so if nothing is done, it will probably die out.

The greater fairy armadillo only grows from 140 to 175 millimeters—it is a very small animal compared to those such as the giant armadillo, or even the nine-banded armadillo. This is the main reason it has the word 'fairy' in its name.

It lives in a very small area of the aforementioned countries, at a spot where they all touch.

Not a lot is known about it, expect that it tunnels a lot and spends much of its time in shallow burrows. We don't know for sure what it eats, or how it goes about reproducing, or much else. It is a rare animal, and not easily spotted.

What we do know is that it is threatened, and that something must be done to save it.

Giant armadillo

The giant armadillo looks like it came right out of an Ice Age movie. It does not curl up at all, its bony plates not allowing it such movement. It has a plate on top of its head, looking much like a hat of some kind.

The giant armadillo is probably the largest kind of armadillo, barring possible extinct ones. The armadillo in general has been around a long time, and the giant armadillo really reflects this fact.

It has huge front claws, and yellow-gray-pink kind of color going on, though all in very dull shades. It is definitely not a brightly-colored creature.

The largest known giant armadillo, which was in captivity, weighed a whopping 80 kilograms!

Giant armadillos eat mainly ants and termites, and because of their size, have been known to eat entire colonies of termites. They are solitary creatures, and fairly nocturnal.

These armadillos are very important to their ecosystem, because they dig tunnels and burrows that other animals often end up living in. Because they are vulnerable to extinction, meaning that they are a little

—

bit in danger, the question has been what will happen to these other animals if they disappear from their habitat.

As captive animals, they sleep about eighteen hours a day. Not a lot is known about them in the wild, and a not completely grown up giant armadillo has never been captured.

We don't know how they go about reproducing either. Chances are, they do some similar things to other armadillos we know about, but there haven't been a lot of studies done on giant armadillos to find out.

The problem for giant armadillos is that they're a good source of meat. The indigenous peoples have hunted them for a very long time, and some even rely very heavily on the giant armadillo for food. Because of its habitat being destroyed, this hunting, and poaching, there is said to have been a major decrease in its numbers over the last three decades.

If nothing is done to reverse this, it may become more and more endangered as time goes on. There are definitely some protected areas for giant armadillos, however, within the countries they live in.

Screaming hairy armadillo

The screaming hairy armadillo is also known as the crying armadillo, the small hairy armadillo, and the small screaming armadillo. The reason it is called a 'screaming' armadillo is not because it is always screaming. Instead, it's called that because when captured or handled, it squeals a lot.

A screaming hairy armadillo (commons.wikimedia.org)

It is not the only one its genus, but it is a better known one. It's called hairy because, in addition to its armor, it has many bristles on its body.

It gives it a very hairy appearance compared to many other kinds of armadillos.

It's a burrowing armadillo that lives in the more southern part of South America, specifically in Argentina, Bolivia, and Paraguay.

The screaming hairy armadillo generally has many burrows in its territory, and a lot of them have more than one entrance. They like to burrow under shrubs or other plants like that. They are able to live at high and low altitudes, though they tend to prefer shrub land.

It also changes whether or it is diurnal (active during the day) or nocturnal (active during the night) depending on the season. It is diurnal in the winter, and it's nocturnal in the summer.

This armadillo eats a lot of small creatures besides insects too. It eats mice, lizards, and other creatures; it especially eats them during the summer, if you compare it to the winter.

It only carries its babies for a little more than two months. A female armadillo of this kind will have two litters a year, typically.

This type of armadillo is very popular as a source of meat in Bolivia. It's also considered a pest, and is killed by hunting dogs. Lastly, it is very popular as a source for the backs of charangos, the guitar-like instrument mentioned previously.

Despite all this, the screaming hairy armadillo is not endangered, and is in fact doing fairly well.

Pink fairy armadillo

The pink fairy armadillo is perhaps the cutest kind of armadillo. It is also called the pichiciego.

A stuffed pink fairy armadillo (commons.wikimedia.org)

The pink fairy armadillo lives in desert type of areas, much preferring them to forests. It digs burrows, and it's nocturnal. It eats worms, insects, slugs, and sometimes even plant parts. It's not known to eat things like lizards and mice like some of its relatives.

The problem with pink fairy armadillos is that they are not sighted very often, and so no one knows for sure if they're endangered or not. The thought is that they are hunted by dogs and cats, people's pets, which are not native to the area. Pink fairy armadillos haven't been sighted as frequently as they used to be.

Conclusion

Armadillos are interesting creatures that live in South, Central, and even North America. They are fascinating to see at zoos, though most of them are rarely seen in the wild.

The armadillo is a hardy creature that has stood the test of time; let's hope they last for thousands, if not millions, more years.

Author Bio

Rachel Smith is a young author who enjoys animals. Once, she had a rabbit who was very nervous, and chewed through her leash and tried to escape. She's also had several pet mice, who were the funniest little animals to watch. She lives in Ohio with her family and writes in her spare time.

Publisher

JD-Biz Corp

P O Box 374

Mendon, Utah 84325

http://www.jd-biz.com/

Mendon Cottage Books
P O Box 374, Mendon Utah 84325

Horses

For Kids

Amazing Animal Books
For Young Readers
By John and
Annalee Davidson

Ponies

For Kids

AmazingAnimalBooks
Rachel Smith

Ten Amazing Horses For Kids

Nature Books for Kids
JD-Biz Publishing
K. Bennett

Akhal-Teke
"The Golden Horse of the desert"
For Kids

Nature Books for Kids
JD-Biz Publishing
K. Bennett

Suffolk-Punch
"The Gentle Giant"
For Kids

Nature Books for Kids
JD-Biz Publishing
K. Bennett

Shires
"The great Horse"
For Kids

Nature Books for Kids
JD-Biz Publishing
K. Bennett

Colonial Spanish
"Horse of the Americas"
For Kids

Nature Books for Kids
JD-Biz Publishing
K. Bennett

Canadian
"The Little Iron Horse"
For Kids

Nature Books for Kids
JD-Biz Publishing
K. Bennett

Cleveland Bays
"History and Future"
Horses For Kids

Nature Books for Kids
JD-Biz Publishing
K. Bennett

Made in the USA
Columbia, SC
06 September 2020